The World of DOGS

Written by Rebecca Blankenhorn

STECK-VAUGHN
ELEMENTARY · SECONDARY · ADULT · LIBRARY

A Harcourt Classroom Education Company

www.steck-vaughn.com

Contents

The Dog World

From the tiny toy poodle to the huge Great Dane, dogs come in many shapes, sizes, and colors. Each **breed**, or kind, of dog has special features. For example, the chow-chow has a black tongue. The pug has a black face. The Dalmatian is white with dark spots.

The cocker spaniel has floppy ears and long fur. The boxer has short hair and ears that stand up.

The borzoi and the Yorkshire terrier have different shapes.

The shape of many dogs allows them to do special things. A borzoi has a long, thin body and legs. It was once used to hunt wolves and other animals because it can run fast. But a borzoi is not very cuddly. Which would you rather have sit in your lap—a borzoi or a Yorkshire terrier?

Even though many breeds of dogs look very different from each other, they are all mammals. They all have similar skeletons, and they are all **carnivores**, or meat-eaters. Like other mammals (including people), dogs feed their babies milk and have hair or fur to keep them warm.

Most dogs have very sharp senses of smell and hearing. They can hear very high sounds that we can't. Their sense of smell is almost a million times better than ours.

Not all dogs are **purebred**. Many are mutts, or mixed-breed dogs. Some mutts are born to parents of different breeds. Many are born to parents that are mixed-breed dogs themselves. Mutts can look and act like purebred dogs. They make great pets.

Mixed-breed dogs come in every size, shape, and color.

American Kennel Club Dog Groups

Working Dogs Working dogs were developed to help people. Alaskan malamutes are used to pull sleds through ice and snow.

Sporting Dogs Sporting dogs began as helpers for people who hunt birds. Sporting dogs include

setters, pointers, retrievers, and spaniels. The golden retriever is one kind of sporting dog.

Hounds Hounds also began as hunting dogs. Some breeds can hunt by following an animal's smell. Others can hunt by following an animal with their eyes. The dachshund (DAHKS hoond) came from Germany. Its name means "badger hound." The dachshund is now kept mainly as a pet.

Terriers Terriers are now often used as watchdogs. They started as hunting dogs. Most terriers have a wiry coat and bushy face hair. The Cairn terrier came from Scotland.

Toy Dogs Toy dogs are small dogs. They were developed to keep people company. Toy dogs come from all over the world. The Chihuahua (chih WAH wah) is one kind of toy dog.

Nonsporting Dogs Nonsporting dogs are like toy dogs. They are kept as pets. Many began as sporting dogs and working dogs. The bulldog is one kind of nonsporting dog.

Herding Dogs Herding dogs were developed to keep sheep or cattle together and protect them. The Old English sheepdog is one of the largest herding dogs.

7

Dogs can be less than 6 inches high (15 centimeters) to almost 4 feet (120 centimeters) tall. They can weigh anywhere from just a few pounds to more than 200 pounds (91 kilograms). Most dogs live between 8 and 15 years. Small dogs often live longer than large dogs.

How Tall Is a Dog?

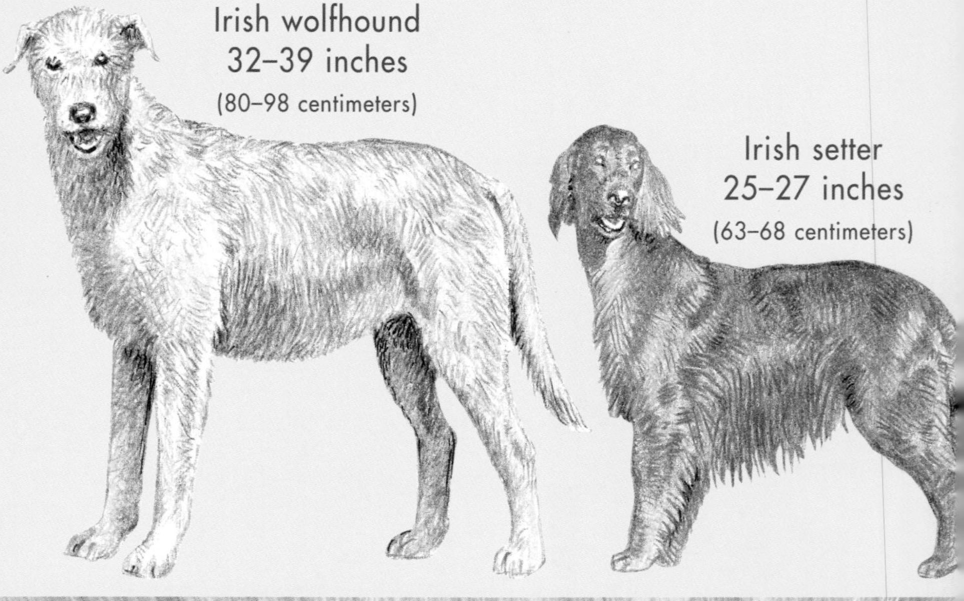

Irish wolfhound
32–39 inches
(80–98 centimeters)

Irish setter
25–27 inches
(63–68 centimeters)

The heaviest and longest dog ever recorded was an Old English mastiff named Zorba. He weighed 343 pounds (156 kilograms) and measured 8 feet, 3 inches (243 centimeters) from the tip of his nose to the end of his tail. Other giants of the dog world include St. Bernards, Newfoundlands, Great Danes, and Irish wolfhounds.

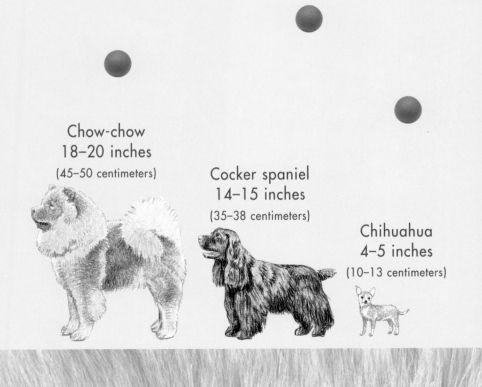

Chow-chow
18–20 inches
(45–50 centimeters)

Cocker spaniel
14–15 inches
(35–38 centimeters)

Chihuahua
4–5 inches
(10–13 centimeters)

Have you ever heard the saying "You can't teach an old dog new tricks"? That really isn't true. But puppies can be easier to train than adult dogs. It is hard for an adult dog to change bad habits, just as it is for people.

Almost all dogs can be trained to work and to obey commands. One reason why dogs are easier to train than cats is that dogs are **social** animals. They want to be with a group. When they are in a group, they try to get along with the others. When dogs think of people as part of their group, they will cooperate with and obey people.

This circus dog is being trained to jump through hoops.

Like people, dogs have different personalities. They can be shy, grouchy, active, friendly, nervous, and even silly. Most dogs are very playful. They usually enjoy games they can play with other dogs or with people, such as tug-of-war and fetch. Some dogs love to swim. Others hate getting wet.

Dogs yawn, just as people do.

Do dogs see in color?

Yes, dogs see color, but not quite the same colors as people do. When we give a dog a bright red ball, it probably sees a pale pink ball.

Some dogs have been the favorites of kings and queens. About 200 years ago, the cuddly Pekingese (pee kuh NEEZ) was a lap dog of the royal palace in Peking, China. In the 1500s King Charles II of England had his favorite dogs named after him. This breed is now known as the King Charles spaniel.

King Charles II with his spaniels.

In England today Queen Elizabeth II keeps Welsh corgis at Buckingham Palace. Corgis have very short legs and were once used to herd cattle. French and English kings and queens of the 1800s had Dalmatians to run beside their carriages. Most German castles had a pair of huge Great Danes as guard dogs.

CHAPTER 2

Show Dogs and Athletes

The first dog show was held in England in 1859. Today different breeds of dogs even have their own clubs. The American Kennel Club keeps records on about 140 different breeds of dogs. It sets up shows that are contests for puppies and adult dogs. Children can show dogs in special events for young people.

Dog shows have different kinds of contests. In some, people walk with their dog around a ring. Judges watch and grade the dogs. The best-looking, best-behaved dogs win first-place ribbons.

A dog-show judge looks at how well the dogs behave.

Some dogs are athletes that compete in important sports events. Dog-sled racing is one of these sports. The first real dog-sled race was the All-Alaska Sweepstakes race in 1908. Before that, sled dogs were used mainly for work in the snowy, cold north.

The most famous dog-sled race today is the 1150-mile Iditarod in Alaska. Every year men and women use sled dogs to go from Nome to Anchorage. This freezing trip takes about 9 days.

The most common sled dogs that the racers use are Alaskan malamutes and Siberian huskies. The Alaskan malamute breed was started by the Inuit people. Siberian huskies were first used for herding reindeer and pulling loads.

In the Iditarod, dogs must race through snow and over ice.

The whippet looks delicate, but it is really strong and powerful.

Greyhounds and whippets are racing dogs. Greyhounds are the fastest dogs on earth. They are able to sprint up to 35 miles (56 kilometers) per hour. That's about 2 times as fast as a person can run! Long ago greyhounds were prized as hunters because they could chase fast **prey**, such as rabbits. Over the years these swift dogs became just as valuable for their speed as for their hunting skills.

Why do some dogs have floppy ears?
Some dogs have straight ears that stand up. Straight ears help them hear sounds better. Dogs with floppy ears often depend more on sight and smell than on hearing.

Hunting is another sport that dogs take part in. Some hounds are specially trained to hunt with people on horseback. Hounds are usually medium to large dogs, but they all have droopy ears. Depending on the breed, they hunt either by sight or by smell. Many have a deep, loud voice.

Setters, pointers, retrievers, and spaniels are other kinds of hunting dogs. These dogs are most often used to hunt birds. They do different jobs for hunters. Both setters and pointers find the prey and "point" at it for the hunter. Spaniels scare it out into the open. Retrievers help hunters by fetching birds that the hunters shoot.

Pointers are trained to stand very still and aim their body at birds.

Retrievers are usually good swimmers because they often have to bring ducks and other birds in from water. They are known as very gentle dogs because they don't crush the prey in their mouth as some hunting dogs do. Many people keep retrievers as pets.

Many of today's favorite pets were once used for hunting. Terriers began as hunters of animals that live underground. The word *terrier* means "earth dog." These dogs were especially good at finding and digging out animals such as rabbits. In addition, terriers were not huge dogs, so hunters could easily keep up with them when hunting on foot. The tiny Australian and Yorkshire terriers once hunted mice and other small **rodents**. Then and now, terriers have plenty of energy and can be very fierce.

Other dogs that began as hunting dogs include cocker spaniels and poodles. Cocker spaniels were used to scare birds called woodcocks into the open. Poodles retrieved ducks for hunters in France.

CHAPTER 3

Dog Detectives and Other Working Dogs

Every day dogs around the world get up and go to work. They don't sit at computers in office buildings. They don't drive tractors on farms. But their strength, speed, bark, loyalty, and sense of smell make them a great help to people. Dogs work at many different jobs, from police work to taking care of other animals.

This beagle has been trained to sniff out termites in the wood of people's homes.

TERMITE DETECTION DOG

Some dogs work to fight crime. In many countries they are members of the police force. Police dogs were first used in the 1700s, but some of the best police dogs came from Germany in the early 1900s. The German shepherd is the most common police dog.

Police dogs learn how to guard a prisoner and catch a running suspect. They learn to be steady and calm during gunfire. Some learn to use their sense of smell to find criminals or drugs. One Labrador retriever named Snag made 118 drug finds worth $810 million. Other police dogs are trained to sniff for bombs.

Police dogs live with their police officer partner. When a police dog reaches 8 to 10 years old, it often does not have to work anymore. It stays home and enjoys life with its partner.

Like police dogs, tracking and rescue dogs use their sense of smell. Because bloodhounds have the best nose of all dogs, they are probably the best tracking dogs. Their super sense of smell can be *3 million* times better than a person's!

Rescue dogs are trained to find people. They can locate people buried under snow or rocks. They can also find lost people who are out in the open. St. Bernards and Bernese mountain dogs are well known as rescue dogs, especially in snowy mountain areas. Long ago these dogs would stay with stranded travelers through the cold night. They kept the people warm until help arrived. One St. Bernard named Barry is famous for rescuing at least 40 people in Switzerland.

A big grave stone marks Barry's resting place.

Throughout history dogs have been used to guard and protect people. Guard dogs are used today by both families and companies. Rottweilers (RAHT wy luhrz), Doberman pinschers (PIHN shuhrz), German shepherds, and mastiffs are the most common kinds of guard dogs today.

This Doberman pinscher's job is to guard an auto repair shop.

Why do dogs sniff everything?

Smelling is the main way that most dogs get information. They can often smell whether another dog or animal has been around. They can smell how long ago it was there. They can even tell whether the other dog was a male or a female and whether it was a puppy or an adult dog.

Labrador retrievers make good seeing-eye dogs.

Seeing-eye dogs, or guide dogs, are working dogs, too. They act as the eyes of people who cannot see. Guide dogs wear a special handle for their owner to hold. A person with a guide dog can go to stores, restaurants, banks, and anywhere else that dogs usually cannot go.

Learning to be a seeing-eye dog is hard work. Seeing-eye dogs begin their training almost as soon as they are born. The dogs must learn to find their way on sidewalks, streets, and stairs. They must learn to avoid dangers that might hurt their owner. They must also learn to ignore all **distractions** while doing their work. The breeds most often used as guide dogs are retrievers and German shepherds.

Hearing dogs help people who cannot hear. A hearing dog is trained to respond to important sounds, such as a smoke alarm, a ringing telephone, a crying baby, and its owner's name. The dog goes back and forth from its owner to the sound until the owner follows.

Another dog that helps people carry on their daily life is the service dog. This dog fetches and moves things for people. It picks up things that drop and gets things from shelves. It turns on light switches, pulls a wheelchair, and carries things. It even goes for help if necessary.

This service dog has been trained to open a refrigerator and fetch things from it.

The Maremma is one kind of herding dog.

Many working dogs take care of other animals. Herding dogs of long ago kept wolves and wild dogs from attacking the herd and kept the herd animals together. Herding dogs of today still work very hard. Border collies, shelties, Welsh corgis, and Belgian shepherds are among the many breeds of herding dogs.

Maremmas are big white guard dogs for sheep. These dogs do not herd the sheep. Instead, they think they are part of the herd! Why? As puppies, Maremmas are sometimes raised with lambs. They start to think of the sheep as family. Adult Maremmas will protect sheep from bears, wolves, and coyotes.

Dogs and Humans

People and dogs have lived together for more than 10,000 years. It's easy to understand why someone living now would love a cute little dachshund or even a big St. Bernard. But did you know that the dachshund, the St. Bernard, and all other tame dogs probably came from the gray wolf? Scientists think that the gray wolf is the closest **ancestor** of all modern dogs.

The gray wolf is also called the timber wolf and the Arctic wolf.

Because all dogs came from wolves, the first **domesticated** dogs looked like wolves. Nobody knows for sure how these dogs were tamed. Perhaps they were hungry, and people fed them. People may also have captured and raised some of the puppies.

About 4000 years ago, people started to create different dog breeds. People all across the world tamed dogs. The dogs learned to hunt, herd sheep, and guard their owners. In return humans gave dogs food and shelter.

As time went on, dogs became less like wolves and easier to tame and train. Dogs' intelligence and social behavior made them good companions for people. The dogs learned to see humans as a group that they could belong to.

Why do dogs pant?

Dogs pant in order to keep cool. People sweat to stay cool, but dogs can't sweat like we do. They can only sweat through their paws.

Ancient Egyptians used dogs to hunt ostriches.

The most common dog seen in ancient Egyptian art seems to be a kind of hound, perhaps like a greyhound. The art shows that the Egyptian people used the hounds for hunting. They also had guard dogs and war dogs.

Dogs were very important to the people of Egypt. They were a part of everyday life. Like today, some dogs lived as strays. Others were well cared for. To make sure their dogs were happy after death, some loving dog owners even had their dogs mummified, or preserved, in nearly the same way that humans were!

Why do dogs turn in circles before lying down?

Before dogs were pets, they all lived out in the wild. When dogs turn in circles, they may be following an instinct to trample the ground and make a comfortable place to rest.

A smart dog with keen hearing, the Lhasa apso makes a great pet.

Today's mastiffs had relatives in Assyria (uh SIHR ee uh). Assyria was a country near what is now Iraq. These huge dogs were used for hunting and warfare. Drawings on huge stone tablets show dogs marching fiercely alongside soldiers.

Ancient Asian people kept a variety of dogs. Lap dogs were very popular with the rich. Hunting and war dogs also were bred in some Asian countries. The fuzzy chow-chow and the Pekingese began in China. The large, bold Akita started as a Japanese war dog. In Tibet many people kept the little Lhasa apso (LAH sa AHP soh) as a guard dog. These loyal little dogs barked loudly when a stranger came near. They still do! Today many people keep Lhasa apsos as pets.

The ancient Romans raised little lap dogs, large war dogs, guard dogs, hounds, and herding dogs. Columella was a Roman who wrote about how to farm. He said that white dogs should be used to guard sheep. That way, shepherds would not mistake the dog for a wolf in the middle of the night! As their art and writing show, dogs were an important part of Romans' lives.

This Roman art is a sign that means "Beware of dog."

Dogs have been part of our lives for many years. They have become our helpers and our friends. In turn, we have taken care of them. Dogs are often so close to us that they become family members. They are soft, furry animals to hold and play with. Dogs also show that they like us. A wagging tail when we come near is a dog's way of smiling at us.

Dogs are very loyal and trusting. They are also protective. This may be why **prehistoric** people used dogs to guard against wild creatures.

Dogs and people have become close friends.

The Howl of the Wild

When we think of dogs, we usually think of the domesticated dog. But *dog* is also the name of a family of animals, and not all are tame. The dog family is also called the **canine** family. Wolves, coyotes, jackals, foxes, and wild dogs are all members of the dog family.

A few canines, such as the bush badger, don't look much like dogs at all. Hyenas look and act as if they might be canines. They really belong to a different family of animals.

The racoon dog belongs to the canine family.

How did the dog family start? We have learned about dog family ancestors by looking at fossils. One of the first canine ancestors was Cynodictis (sin oh DIK tus). It lived about 40 million years ago. Cynodictus was a meat-eater and looked like a weasel.

About 300,000 years ago, Cynodictis began to die out. Wolves then began to develop. During the Ice Age, dire wolves roamed across North America. These prehistoric wolves were bigger than any wolf that lives today. Bones of dire wolves have been found in tar pits in California. Like other animals, dire wolves got stuck in the tar pits. Their bones remained there for thousands of years.

The dire wolf had huge teeth.

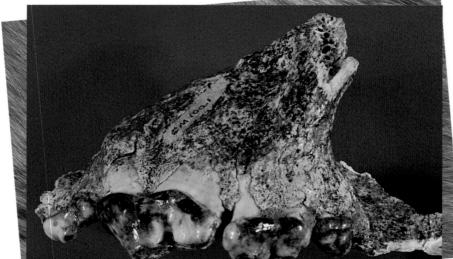

Long ago there were many more wolves than there are now. For example, the European wolf once lived all across Europe. Only a few of them now live there. Why are there fewer wolves now? Hate and fear have led people to kill many wolves. Many people hate wolves because wolves eat farm animals. Some people believe that wolves will attack humans.

The red wolf is smaller than the gray wolf.

Do dogs dream?

Dogs do dream, but we really have no idea what they dream about. Some even snore. You can tell when a dog is dreaming. Watch for kicking or noises while it sleeps.

The United States has listed the gray wolf as an endangered animal in almost every state. The red wolf is endangered in all the southern states.

Mother wolves spend much time with their pups.

Wolves live in groups called **packs**, and baby wolves are called pups. Wolves howl to talk to one another, and they work together when they hunt. Each pack usually has one male and female that lead the others. Pups play at fighting so that they can learn to hunt.

Wolves usually kill and eat animals that are weak or sick. They will eat birds and rodents when there is nothing else to eat. In the wild, wolves are very shy and stay away from people.

Two other dog relatives are the coyote and the jackal. The coyote lives mostly in North America. Smaller than a wolf, the coyote is a hunter and **scavenger**. Coyotes usually live in pairs or in a family group, but they hunt in larger packs. Farmers and ranchers do not like coyotes because coyotes sometimes kill their sheep and chickens. Hungry coyotes also ruin crops—even watermelon!

Coyotes have begun to live in and near cities. They make messes when they get into trash cans. They also hurt people's pets.

The jackal is slightly smaller than the coyote. Jackals live throughout Africa, southern Europe, and Asia. Like wolves, both jackals and coyotes can be heard howling at night.

The jackal looks like a fox.

Foxes are members of the canine family. But they don't howl at all. Foxes are quiet loners with pointed noses and thick, bushy tails. They hunt on their own, and they usually eat rabbits and other rodents. They eat insects, too.

Foxes are smaller than coyotes and jackals. They are found in many different **habitats**, from the Arctic to the desert. The most common fox is the red fox. It, too, can be found in cities.

Some members of the dog family are known as wild dogs. The dingo is one kind of wild dog. Dingoes live in Australia. They were the only dogs there for hundreds of years. Dingoes were also tame but have become wild again. They hunt together in packs and act more like wolves than like dogs.

Do all canines bark?

Some canines, like wolves and foxes, rarely bark, but all canines can make "woof" noises. They can whine and howl and growl. The Basenji is a dog that came from Africa. It does not bark, but sometimes it yelps.

The DOG & the Shadow

IS image the Dog did not know,
Or his bone's, in the pond's painted show:
" T'other dog," so he thought,
" Has got more than he ought;"
So he snapped, & his dinner saw go!

GREED IS SOMETIMES
CAUGHT BY ITS
OWN BAIT

Aesop used dogs in several of his fables.

Many stories have been written about dogs. Aesop's fable "The Wolf and the Dog" tells of a hungry wolf that asks a dog for help. The dog offers the wolf a place in his master's home. On the way, the wolf sees that the dog wears a collar. The wolf decides that he would rather be free than comfortable.

Some stories tell of dogs' loyalty to people. In one old story, a man kills his loyal Irish wolfhound. The man made a mistake and thought that the dog had hurt his baby son. But the wolfhound had really saved the boy by killing a wolf.

Dogs are main characters in many famous books, too. *The Incredible Journey* tells the story of two dogs and a cat who make a long trip to get back to their home. In *The Call of the Wild* and *White Fang*, dogs of the cold north perform many brave deeds.

Dogs are also characters in movies and TV shows. Some dogs have become famous from their TV and movie roles. People recognize these dogs just as they do human movie stars.

Dogs are often used in TV commercials.

Glossary

ancestor a relative from very long ago

breed a group of dogs that have the same features

canine a member of the dog family, which includes wolves, jackals, coyotes, foxes, and domesticated dogs

carnivore a meat-eater

distraction anything that keeps the mind from staying on task

domesticated tamed and kept by humans

habitat the natural place where an animal lives

pack a group

prehistoric in the time before events were written down

prey an animal that is hunted by another animal for food

purebred having a mother, father, and ancestors of the same breed

rodent a small gnawing or nibbling mammal, such as a mouse

scavenger an animal that feeds on dead animals or plants

social liking to be with others

Index